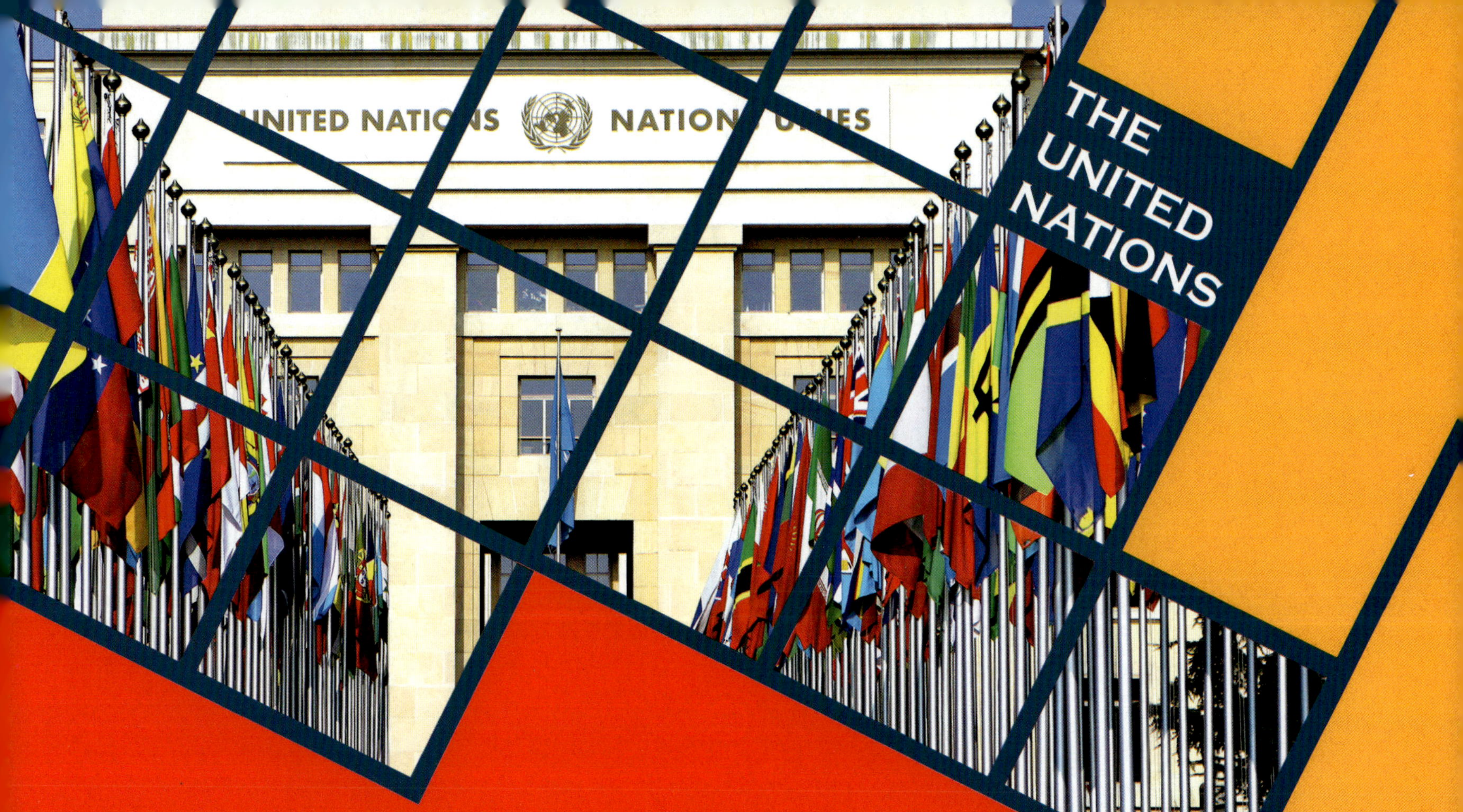

THE UNITED NATIONS

# THE BIRTH OF THE UN, DECOLONIZATION, AND BUILDING STRONG NATIONS

BY SHEILA NELSON AND SARA CUCINI



TEACHER RESOURCES

LIGHTBOX
openlightbox.com

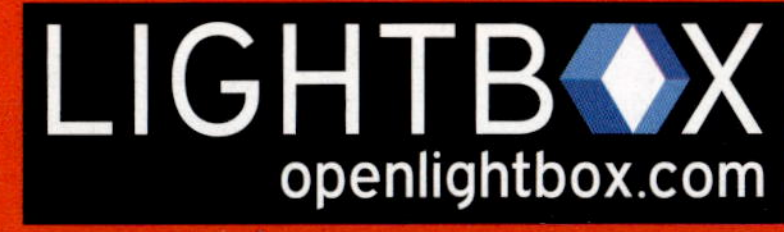

Lightbox is an all-inclusive digital solution for the teaching and learning of curriculum topics in an original, groundbreaking way. Lightbox is based on National Curriculum Standards.

## STANDARD FEATURES OF LIGHTBOX

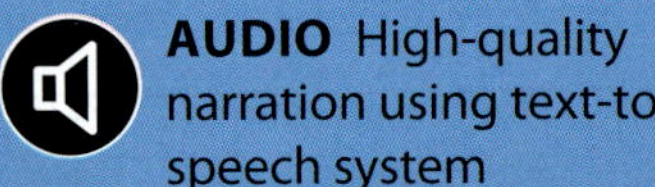
**AUDIO** High-quality narration using text-to-speech system

**VIDEOS** Embedded high-definition video clips

**ACTIVITIES** Printable PDFs that can be emailed and graded

**WEBLINKS** Curated links to external, child-safe resources

**SLIDESHOWS** Pictorial overviews of key concepts

**TRANSPARENCIES** Step-by-step layering of maps, diagrams, charts, and timelines

**INTERACTIVE MAPS** Interactive maps and aerial satellite imagery

**QUIZZES** Ten multiple choice questions that are automatically graded and emailed for teacher assessment

**KEY WORDS** Matching key concepts to their definitions

**MORE** Extra information and details on the subject

**FIRST HAND** Letters, diaries, and other primary sources

**DOCS** Speeches, newspaper articles, and other historical documents

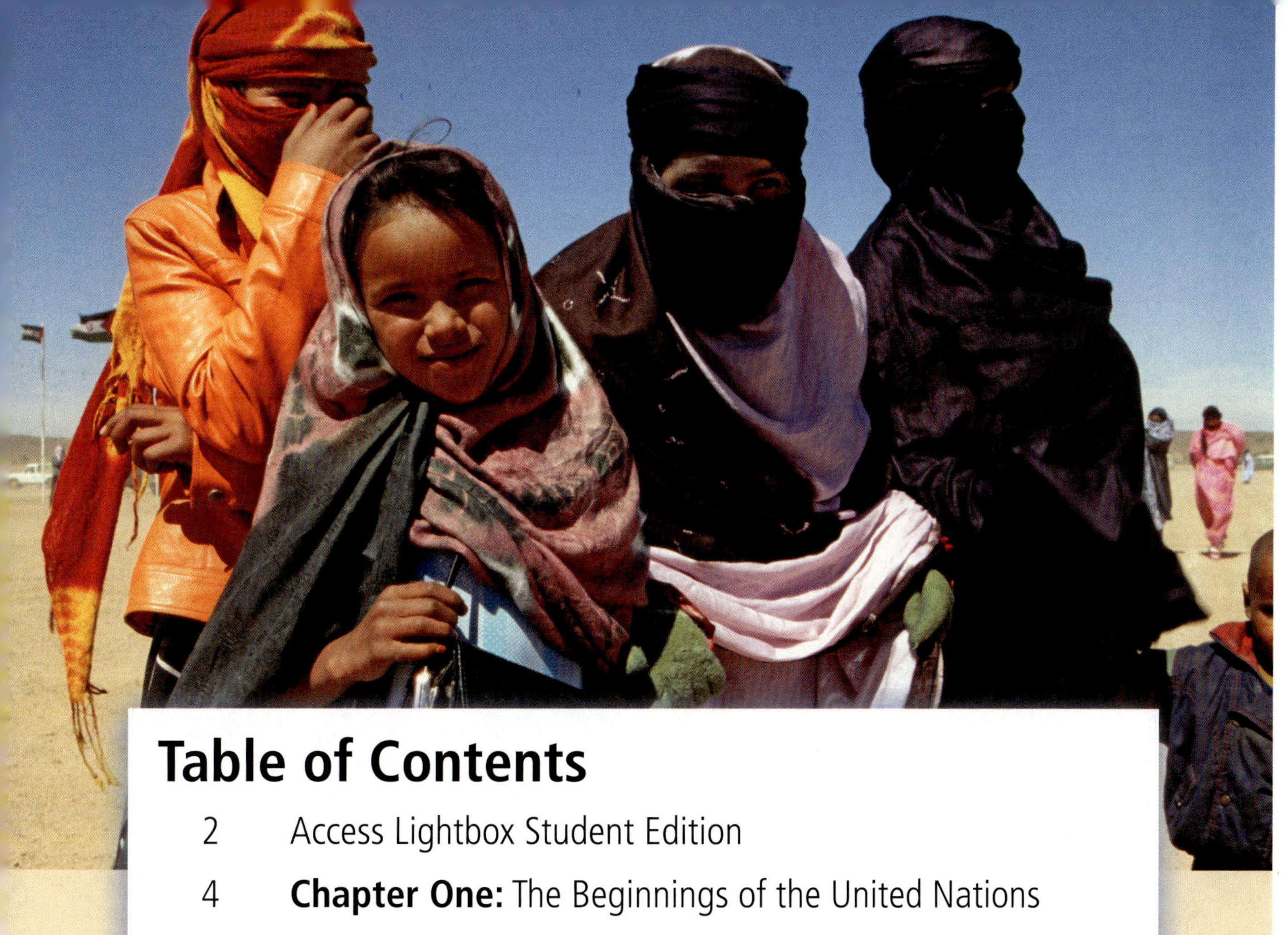

# Table of Contents

**RUBRIC**

## Analyzing a Video

**Students will watch and assess a video related to an event or topic, and write an analysis of the video. An exemplary video analysis will meet the following criteria.**

- Identifies the purpose of the video
- Identifies the intended audience of the video
- Identifies the video as a primary or secondary source
- Discusses the historical and social context of the video
- Describes how the content of the video is presented
- Summarizes the information and opinions presented in the video
- Analyzes the quality of the content presented in the video
- Assesses the effectiveness of the video
- Determines whether the images and graphics used in the video relate to the content
- Determines whether the video is easy to follow and understand
- Gives the analysis a clear and consistent purpose
- Organizes the analysis in a logical, effective manner
- Presents a strong, clear argument about the video
- Provides strong and accurate details to support the argument about the video
- Considers other perspectives on the purpose and effectiveness of the video
- Cites all sources used in the analysis

# CHAPTER 1

The five Allied powers—the United States, the United Kingdom, the Soviet Union, France, and China—met in London during World War II to discuss what a peaceful world would look like after the war was over.

# The Beginnings of the United Nations

As World War II raged in Europe and Asia, leaders of the **Allied** countries met often to talk about war strategies—and to figure out how to make sure a similar war never happened again. During these meetings, they decided to form an organization of nations, an organization that would work for peace and help the peoples of the world live better lives. The Allied leaders felt a large group of countries actively working to bring about peace and world development would be able to prevent future world wars and the spreading power of tyrannical dictators such as Adolf Hitler.

In 1945, **delegates** from 50 countries met in San Francisco, California, and drew up a charter for the United

**75**
The number of internationally recognized independent, self-governing states in the world in 1919, the year after World War I ended and the year the League of Nations was founded.

**72**
The number of internationally recognized independent, self-governing states in 1945, the year that World War II ended and the United Nations was founded.

**195**
The number of internationally recognized independent, self-governing states in the world as of 2017.

**ACTIVITIES**

**First Hand**

**Lessons of Second World War Must Continue to Guide United Nations Work**

Examine the legacy of World War II and its influence on the work of the United Nations.

1. How are World War II and the United Nations linked? How did the delegates describe this connection? Support your answer with excerpts from the text.
2. In the words of the delegates, how had the world situations changed since the end of World War II? What action did they suggest to allow the United Nations to adapt to these changes? Why?

**Video**

**San Francisco Conference**

Analyze the 1945 newsreel about the UN conference of San Francisco.

1. How does the video introduce the topic of the conference? How is the conference described? Why is it described in these terms?
2. Would a modern news report about the conference be similar or different? How would it be similar? How would it be different?

**RUBRIC**

## Analyzing a Primary Source

**Students will complete a thorough analysis of a primary source. An exemplary analysis will meet the following criteria.**

- Identifies the creator of the source
- Explains what medium was used to create the primary source
- Describes why the source qualifies as a primary one
- Explores any literary devices used in the source
- Identifies the intended audience for the source
- Relates the creator's goals in creating the source
- Illustrates knowledge of the period and location in which the source was created
- Distinguishes between facts and opinions found in the source
- Examines the reliability of the source's creator
- Compares the source with similar documents
- Cites additional sources used in the analysis
- Presents information in a clear, concise manner
- Uses correct spelling, grammar, and punctuation

Edward R. Stettinius, Jr. (right), was the U.S. ambassador to the United Nations in 1945 and 1946. Part of his role was to report back to President Harry Truman.

Nations (UN). The Charter listed the purposes of the organization as:

1. To maintain international peace and security.
2. To develop friendly relationships among nations based on respect for the principle of equal rights and **self-determination** of peoples.
3. To achieve international cooperation in solving international problems.

Representatives from 51 countries (the 50 who had met in San Francisco, plus Poland, who had not been able to attend the convention) signed the Charter, showing their approval and support of the organization.

On October 24, 1945, the United Nations officially began its existence after the five permanent Security Council members—the United States, the United Kingdom, the Soviet Union (now Russia), France, and China—**ratified** its charter.

### The League of Nations

The United Nations was not the first international organization. After World War I, 42 countries formed a similar group, called the League of Nations. The League of Nations had been the idea of U.S. president Woodrow Wilson, and its goals were very much like those of the later United Nations. The League wanted to prevent another war and make the world a better place for all people.

Unfortunately, the League had a number of problems from its founding in 1919. One problem was that the United States never joined the organization, preferring to focus on national interests, in spite of the fact the idea behind the League of Nations came from an American leader. With one of the major world powers missing, the League never had the power it could have wielded.

Another problem was that so many countries wanted to avoid war at any cost. Although this looked like a good thing, it meant that the countries of the League of Nations, such as the United Kingdom and France, preferred to avoid confrontations with tyrants rather than enforce **economic sanctions** against, for example, the growing threat of Nazi Germany.

Probably the most serious problem facing the League of Nations was that any decision made by the League Council had to be approved by all the members. Since the Council was made up of 9 to 15 members—at different times—**unanimous** decisions were nearly impossible, meaning very little was actually accomplished.

World War II began in 1939, and the League of Nations had not been able to prevent it. The member countries knew the League had failed in its primary purpose—to prevent war—and the League Assembly and Council did not meet at all during World War II.

The United Nations replaced the League of Nations, carrying over many of the same goals and purposes. The new organization began its first official meetings in January of 1946, and the League of Nations was disbanded in April of the same year.

Despite failing to succeed in its primary goal of achieving world peace, the League of Nations brought worldwide attention to issues that continue to be of importance today. These include child labor and other worker-rights concerns, slavery, **epidemics**, the plight of **refugees**, and setting the course for colonies toward

**ACTIVITIES**

**Document**

**UN Charter**

Evaluate the content of the UN Charter.

1. What are the principles the UN "shall act in accordance with"? Why were these principles established? How are the purposes of the UN described in the text? In your opinion, has the UN fulfilled these purposes and respected these principles over time? Justify your answer.
2. Why was the United States chosen to be the repository of the Charter's ratification? Why was the Charter deposited in the archives of the U.S. government?

The League of Nations had a council whose task was to settle disputes. The members of the council met four times a year at a minimum, and could meet additional times as needed.

**self-government** and statehood. The League also helped bring about the birth of the United Nations.

## Decolonization

The United Nations began with general goals of peace and international welfare, but it had specific goals as well. One of these specific objectives was **decolonization**.

European countries had started planting colonies in the sixteenth century, shortly after they discovered the existence of the New World. This was the age of exploration. Explorers traveled all over the world, charting oceans and continents. In the nineteenth century, European colonization increased, as the leaders of the Western world realized the amount of land unclaimed by other industrialized nations was shrinking quickly. Africa, especially, was affected, as European countries rushed to stake claims on the world. The developed countries wanted colonies because of the natural resources and wealth they could bring in to their mother country. Sometimes, colonies provided distant lands where prisoners could be banished—as was the case with Australia in its early years as a British colony.

After World War I, some countries tried to get rid of some of their colonies. The war had been extremely expensive and was followed by the Great Depression. Countries such as the United Kingdom could no longer afford to support a vast empire. At the same time, many colonies were not ready to become independent. These colonies

ACTIVITIES

## Weblink

**The Colonization of Africa**

Analyze how Africa became subjected to colonial domination.

1. What factors pushed European countries to expand their domination over African territory? Do these factors remain important nowadays? Why or why not? If they are still important, how do these factors influence the actions of world countries today?
2. What forms of resistance did African countries adopt? Why did they adopt these particular forms of resistance?

Dahomey, now known as the West African country of Benin, was a French colony for the first half of the twentieth century. It became independent in 1960.

had been ruled by an outside power for so long they needed to be rebuilt from within to regain the tools needed to govern themselves.

## Universal Declaration of Human Rights

One of the most important documents of the United Nations, apart from the Charter, is the Universal Declaration of **Human Rights**, adopted in 1948, which established another specific goal of the United Nations. The Declaration is intended to guide the actions of the United Nations and its member countries, giving an outline of the basic rights all humans should expect.

Although the Declaration is not part of international law, and therefore cannot legally be enforced, all member countries of the United Nations have agreed they will work toward the rights outlined in the Declaration. The countries administering Non-Self-Governing Territories (lands still under colonial control) also agreed to help work toward these rights in their colonies and territories—sometimes a large and difficult task.

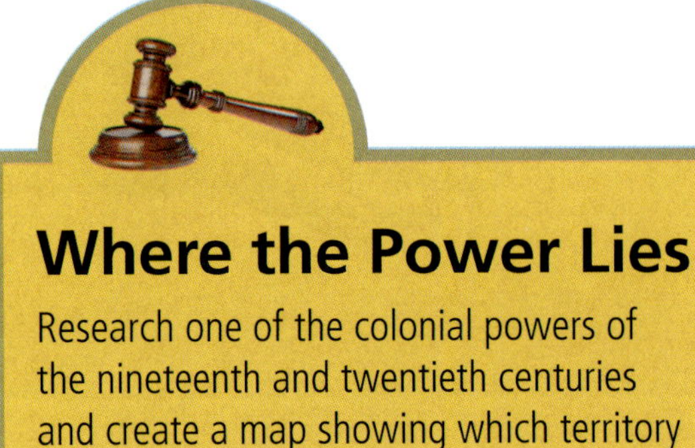

### Where the Power Lies

Research one of the colonial powers of the nineteenth and twentieth centuries and create a map showing which territory or territories it controlled.

## ACTIVITIES

### Document

**Universal Declaration of Human Rights**

Analyze the definition of human rights given by the Universal Declaration of Human Rights.

1. What are the human rights listed in the Declaration? Why are these considered human rights? Justify your answer.
2. What other rights could have been added to the Declaration? Why might one add these rights to the Declaration? Why were these rights not included in the Declaration?

Eleanor Roosevelt, the wife of President Franklin D. Roosevelt, led the 18-member group that was responsible for writing the Universal Declaration of Human Rights.

# CHAPTER 2

The president of Tanganyika, a UN Trust Territory administered by the United Kingdom, met with the British governor of the area before it became an independent country now known as Tanzania.

# The Trusteeship System

After World War II, the Allies had to make many decisions about the countries that had lost the war. One of these decisions involved the colonies of the conquered nations. What should be done with these colonies? Who should look out for their interests until they were ready to become independent?

## Trusteeship Council

At its creation, the United Nations designed a **trusteeship** system to look after the colonies of the **Axis** powers—called **Trust Territories**—and dedicated an entire chapter of the Charter to describing the goals and duties of the system. The Trusteeship Council would oversee the system and would be one of the six main organs of the United Nations. (The others were the General Assembly, the Security Council, the Economic and Social Council, the Secretariat, and the International Court of Justice.) The purpose of the

**14**
The number of Mandates, or colonies formerly belonging to nations defeated during World War I, that were placed under the control of countries in the League of Nations until the colonies were able to become self-governing.

**11**
The number of Trust Territories, some of them post-World War I Mandates and others formerly controlled by losing countries in World War II, that were placed under the control of UN members until they became self-governing.

**0**
The number of Trust Territories that have not achieved some form of self-governance and remain under the control of UN members.

**ACTIVITIES**

**Video**
**The Trusteeship Council**
Examine the purpose and functions of the Trusteeship Council.

1. What are the purposes of the trusteeship system? What is the composition of the Trusteeship Council? Why would this specific composition guarantee the functioning of the trusteeship system?
2. What are the purposes of the Trusteeship Council nowadays? How could this organ be reformed?

**Weblink**
**United Republic of Tanzania: History**
Analyze the history of the United Republic of Tanzania.

1. Which foreign powers controlled Tanzania over the years? What impact might foreign domination have on developing a sense of nationality in the Tanzanian people? Formulate some hypotheses.
2. What is the structure of Tanzania's government? What is its voting system? In your opinion, were these influenced by the colonial past of the country? Why or why not?

**RUBRIC**

## Writing a Comparative Essay

**Students will analyze two topics, and then write a comparative essay based on their analysis. An exemplary comparative essay will meet the following criteria.**

- Consists of a one-paragraph introduction, two or more body paragraphs, and a one-paragraph conclusion
- Introduction includes an engaging lead statement about the topic of the essay, more detailed information about the chosen topic, and a one-sentence thesis that specifically states the essay's argument
- Each body paragraph includes a topic sentence that refers to and supports the thesis, textual evidence of the argument, and an analysis of this evidence
- Body paragraphs end with a transition to the next paragraph
- Conclusion refers to the topic of the essay and the points presented in the body paragraphs, and restates the thesis
- Provides a thorough analysis of the topics in question
- Presents a clear, specific thesis that indicates a high level of critical engagement
- Organizes ideas in a logical manner
- Communicates arguments in a clear, effective manner
- Uses correct spelling, punctuation, and grammar
- Properly integrates any quotations used
- Correctly cites all sources used
- Correctly formats bibliography

Trusteeship Council was to guide the Trust Territories toward self-government. Ideally, this purpose would be quickly fulfilled and the Council would no longer be needed.

The members of the Trusteeship Council are the same as the five permanent members of the Security Council—although the individual representatives are different people. These members are China, France, the Russian Federation, the United Kingdom, and the United States.

## League of Nations Mandates

Just as the United Nations dealt with the issue of what to do with the colonies of their conquered enemies, the League of Nations had faced the same dilemma after World War I. While the United Nations had Trust Territories, the League of Nations had **Mandates**. These Mandates were divided into three groups, based on how ready for self-government the League of Nations believed them to be. Class A Mandates were nearly ready to become independent, and, in fact, all the Class A Mandates had become self-governing by 1949. Class B Mandates were not quite as well developed, and the mandatory powers—the equivalent of the administering powers, or countries, of the Trusteeship Council under the UN—had more control over these

Although Palau is still a territory of the United States, it has its own president.

## League of Nations Mandates and Their Mandatory Powers

**In 1919, following the defeat of Germany and the Ottoman Empire, or present-day Turkey, in World War I, control of their former colonies was transferred to the League of Nations. The colonies were classified according to how ready they were for self-government.**

| Class of Mandate | Mandate | Former Governing Power | New Mandatory Power |
|---|---|---|---|
| A | Syria | Ottoman Empire (Turkey) | France |
| | Lebanon | Ottoman Empire (Turkey) | France |
| | Iraq | Ottoman Empire (Turkey) | United Kingdom |
| | Palestine | Ottoman Empire (Turkey) | United Kingdom |
| | Transjordan | Ottoman Empire (Turkey) | United Kingdom |
| B | Ruanda-Urundi | Germany | Belgium |
| | Togoland | Germany | France<br>United Kingdom |
| | Cameroons | Germany | France<br>United Kingdom |
| | Tanganyika | Germany | United Kingdom |
| C | South West Africa | Germany | South Africa |
| | German Samoa | Germany | New Zealand |
| | New Guinea | Germany | Australia |
| | Nauru | Germany | Australia |
| | German Islands in North Pacific | Germany | Japan |

**ACTIVITIES**

### Weblink

**The League of Nations**

Analyze the evolution of the League of Nations and its relation to the United Nations.

1. What was the purpose of the League of Nations? How was it organized? What improvements to its organization would have made the League of Nations an effective institution?
2. How did the League of Nations differ from the United Nations? Compare and contrast the two organizations.

areas. The mandatory powers had the greatest control over Class C Mandates, and these Mandates essentially became colonies of the mandatory powers. However, in all cases, the mandatory powers were not allowed to build military fortifications or gather armies in the Mandates.

When the League of Nations disbanded, it turned over control of its Mandates to the United Nations. The Mandates then became Trust Territories under the Trusteeship Council, with the goal of helping them all become self-governing.

## The Trust Territories

Many of the 11 Trust Territories were former League of Nations Mandates. Each faced unique situations, but the Trusteeship Council and the administering powers worked with the Trust Territories to help them gain self-government. This could mean independence, or it could mean the people of the territory chose to become part of another country or to become a territory of another country.

In 1960, French Cameroons became the first Trust Territory to achieve independence, as the Republic of Cameroon. In 1961, British Cameroons also became independent, with its northern part joining the nation of Nigeria and its southern part joining the new nation of Cameroon. Also in 1960, the Italian-administered Trust Territory of Somaliland joined a Non-Self-Governing Territory, British Somaliland, to form the independent state of Somalia.

By the late 1960s, six more Trust Territories had become independent.

Several modern buildings have been built in the Cameroon capital of Yaoundé to house its government.

## Trust Territories

**The Trust Territories, their administering powers, and the date and details of their gaining self-government are shown here.**

| Trust Territory | Administering Power | Year of Self-Governance | Notes on Gaining Self-Governance |
|---|---|---|---|
| **French Cameroons (Cameroun)** | France | 1960 | Independence as Cameroon |
| **British Cameroons** | United Kingdom | 1961 | Northern part joined Nigeria, Southern part joined Cameroon |
| **Nauru** | Australia | 1968 | Independence as Nauru |
| **New Guinea** | Australia | 1975 | Joined the Non-Self-Governing Territory of Papua to become the independent state of Papua New Guinea |
| **Ruanda-Urundi** | Belgium | 1962 | Divided into the independent states of Rwanda and Burundi |
| **Somaliland** | Italy | 1960 | Joined the Non-Self-Governing Territory of British Somaliland to become the independent state of Somalia |
| **Tanganyika** | United Kingdom | 1961 | Independence as Tanganyika (in 1964, joined Zanzibar to become Tanzania) |
| **Togoland** | France | 1960 | Independence as Togo |
| **Togoland** | United Kingdom | 1957 | Joined the Non-Self-Governing Territory of the Gold Coast to become the independent state of Ghana |
| **Trust Territory of the Pacific Islands** | United States | | |
| **Federated States of Micronesia** | | 1990 | Self-governing in **free association** with the United States |
| **Republic of the Marshall Islands** | | 1990 | Self-governing in free association with the United States |
| **Commonwealth of the Northern Mariana Islands** | | 1990 | Self-governing as **Commonwealth** of the United States |
| **Palau** | | 1994 | Self-governing in free association with the United States |
| **Western Samoa** | New Zealand | 1962 | Independence as Samoa |

**ACTIVITIES**

### Weblink

**History explains why Cameroon is at war with itself over language and culture.**
Examine the current situation of Cameroon and how this situation is linked to past events.

1. How has the most recent crisis in Cameroon centered on its legal system? Why would having Francophone magistrates in Anglophone regions be an issue?
2. How did colonialism contribute to the current crisis? Did the United Nations' action have an effect on the current crisis in Cameroon? Why or why not?

**RUBRIC**

## Analyzing a Magazine Article

**Students will assess a magazine article and write an analysis. An exemplary analysis will meet the following criteria.**

- Identifies the topic of the article
- Identifies the main points and opinions presented in the article
- Identifies the writer of the article
- Presents information about the writer and infers how his or her life may have shaped this opinion
- Assesses the writer's reliability
- Analyzes how the writer makes his or her argument
- Uses evidence from the article to show how the writer supports his or her argument
- Analyzes the writer's use of literary devices to enhance the article
- Differentiates between facts and opinions presented in the article
- Identifies when and where the article was published, and determines its intended audience
- Identifies and understands the goals of the article
- Assesses the effectiveness of the format in presenting the writer's argument
- Connects the article to the societal and historical context in which it was written
- Infers what is not said about this topic in the article
- Identifies what information is unintentionally implied in the article

In 1975, New Guinea joined the Non-Self-Governing Territory (NSGT) of Papua to become the independent state of Papua New Guinea. The last Trust Territory to gain self-government was Palau, part of the Trust Territory of the Pacific Islands and administered by the United States. Palau became self-governing in 1994—not by seeking independence, but by choosing to be a territory of the United States. When Palau gained self-government, the work of the Trusteeship Council was completed.

## The Future of the Trusteeship Council

On November 1, 1994, the Trusteeship Council had its last meeting. Palau had become self-governing a month before, and the Council's job was done. Although the regulations of the Trusteeship Council stated they must meet at least once a year, the Council decided to change this rule and meet only if necessary.

Although the Trusteeship Council no longer has a job to do, it cannot be completely disbanded without changing the Charter of the United Nations. Also, different people and groups have different ideas about how to deal with the Trusteeship Council. One committee recommended that the Trusteeship Council should take over administration of those areas belonging to no one nation, such as Antarctica, the oceans, the atmosphere, and outer space. On the other hand, former UN secretary-general Kofi Annan stated in March 2005 that he would like to make large changes to the entire structure of the United Nations. One of these would be to eliminate the Trusteeship Council completely. To do so, the UN would have to amend its charter, which has been a sticking point blocking the elimination of the council.

While some people question the effectiveness of the United Nations, the success of the Trusteeship Council is proof that the United Nations has succeeded in at least one area. The Trusteeship Council was given eleven

As a disputed territory, Western Sahara has several groups of people disagreeing on who should rule the area. Sahrawi people currently living in refugee camps in the area believe that it should be governed by the Sahrawi Arab Democratic Republic and protest to show their displeasure.

Trust Territories to administer and help to achieve self-government, and it met this goal in 1994 with the decision of the Palau people to become self-governing.

Although the Trusteeship Council has finished the job it was given, and all the Trust Territories are now self-governing, 16 NSGTs are still working toward independence. The status of a 17th non-self-governing region, Western Sahara, in northwest Africa, has been the object of debate and conflict among several countries and **factions** since Spain withdrew from the territory in 1975–1976.

## Where the Power Lies

Research and write a report on the struggles to become self-governing experienced by one of the UN Trust Territories.

## ACTIVITIES

### Document

**The Alternative UN**

Analyze the magazine article about Kofi Annan's 2005 proposal for the reform of the United Nations.

1. What are Annan's reasons for a proposed reform of the United Nations? Do you think these reasons are valid today? Justify your answer.
2. What changes have been proposed to the Trusteeship Council? In your opinion, had they been implemented, would these changes have been effective? Why or why not?

# CHAPTER 3

Although American Samoa is administered by the United States, it continues to have its own unique culture separate from the mainland.

# Non-Self-Governing Territories

When the United Nations was founded in 1945, most of Africa, parts of Southeast Asia, and many Pacific Islands fell under the category of NSGTs. By 2005, more than 80 of these territories had become self-governing. Today, the number of territories on the list of NSGTs stands at 17.

## Declaration on the Granting of Independence

By 1960, UN membership had grown from the 51 founding members to nearly 100. Many of these new members were countries that had gained their independence in the previous 15 years. Despite the success of the UN's decolonization policies, many countries felt the organization was working too slowly. Dozens of territories were still not self-governing and needed support to achieve independence.

The UN General Assembly discussed the issue of decolonization and decided to put an effort into making it a higher priority. On December 14, 1960, it issued

**2.25 billion**
The approximate world population in 1945, the year the UN was founded.

**750 million**
The number of people living under colonial rule in NSGTs in 1945, which was nearly one-third of the world's population at that time.

**Fewer than 2 million**
The number of people who live in Non-Self-Governing Territories today.

**ACTIVITIES**

**Video**

**Which Countries Still Have Colonies?**
Analyze the situations of various non-self-governing territories.

1. In your opinion, is it correct to define these non-self-governing territories as "colonies"? Support your opinion.
2. Do you agree with the definition of "colony" given by the video? Why are some territories technically falling under this definition not called "colonies"?

**Weblink**

**Non-Self-Governing Territories**
Compare and contrast the Non-Self-Governing Territories.

1. Since when have the different territories been listed as non-self-governing? Which countries administer the non-self-governing territories? Why are these specific countries administering powers?
2. What actions could the UN take nowadays to help these 17 territories become self-governing?

**RUBRIC**

## Holding a Classroom Debate

**Students will form groups and prepare arguments for a debate on a controversial issue. Exemplary performance in a debate will meet the following criteria.**

- Demonstrates in-depth understanding of the topic and related information
- Presents strong, logical, and convincing arguments
- Communicates in a clear and confident manner
- Uses clear vocal inflection and tone
- Uses a reasonable rate of vocal delivery
- Uses respectful and appropriate language and body language
- Delivers arguments, supporting evidence, and counter evidence in an engaging and persuasive manner
- Supports each major point of an argument with several relevant and detailed facts and examples
- Connects all arguments to the overall topic in a clear, concise, and organized manner
- Presents clear, thorough, and accurate information throughout the debate
- Identifies any weakness in the opposing team's arguments
- Presents counter arguments confidently, showing preparation for this component prior to the debate
- Presents strong and persuasive arguments throughout the debate
- Summarizes the arguments in the closing statement

People celebrate Zimbabwe's Independence Day in the capital city of Harare on April 18 each year.

the "Declaration on the granting of independence to colonial countries and peoples," also known as Resolution 1514. This declaration affirmed the right of all peoples to independence, including political freedom to help determine how they are governed.

Also included in the declaration was a section stating that the United Nations was opposed to violent means of bringing about self-government. This was a serious problem in a number of NSGTs, as several groups would sometimes fight for control of the region, and the residents of the territory would become the innocent victims of this battle for power. The goal of the United Nations was to usher in political independence by peaceful means.

### Options for Non-Self-Governing Territories

The day after the General Assembly issued Resolution 1514, it announced another resolution—Resolution 1541. Resolution 1514, the "Declaration on the granting of independence to colonial countries and peoples," had asserted the rights of all peoples to self-government. It also confirmed that the United Nations was to help bring about these rights for all NSGTs. Now, Resolution 1541 gave three options for

NSGTs to determine their own form of governance. Such a territory could become self-governing by doing one of the following:

1. becoming an independent country,
2. choosing to link itself with another independent country, or
3. choosing to become a part of another independent country.

Whatever the people of an NSGT chose, the important thing was that it was their decision, not one forced on them by violence or fear. Sometimes, the people chose for their territory to become associated with another country, with the option of becoming an independent country in the future.

## The Process of Becoming Independent

Every NSGT is administered by another country. For a territory to reach the point at which it is ready to become self-governing, it needs the full support of the administering nation. The exact process of becoming self-governing is different for each territory, since each faces a unique set of circumstances. Each case has to be examined individually to develop a plan with steps leading to self-government.

One of the most important concerns to be dealt with before a territory can become self-governing is violence and oppression. If, for example, two factions are fighting for control of a territory, the people will not feel safe enough to make necessary steps toward self-government.

When people are being terrorized, they are not free to make decisions about their future. Political candidates might face the threat of assassination, and residents could be intimidated into voting a certain way. In this case, the fact that the territory held an election would not necessarily mean the will of the people had been done. Resolution 1514 states,

*"All armed action or repressive measures of all kinds directed against dependent peoples shall cease in order to enable them to exercise peacefully and freely their right to complete independence, and the integrity of their national territory shall be respected."*

Of course, a territory does not have to be perfect and have solved all its problems before it can become self-governing; all countries have complex issues they must deal with. In fact, the

The Democratic Republic of the Congo, which gained independence in 1960, faced political unrest for many years after. Military forces patrolled towns during the 2011 presidential election, the second in the country's history.

**ACTIVITIES**

### Document

**Declaration on the Granting of Independence to Colonial Countries and Peoples**

Analyze the text of the Resolution 1514.

1. Do you agree with the statement "the continued existence of colonialism prevents the development of international economic co-operation" and "impedes the social, cultural and economic development of dependent peoples"? Why or why not? Why is colonialism an impediment to economic co-operation"? How does it impede social, cultural, and economical development?
2. Why might partial or total disruption of the national unity and territorial integrity of a country be "incompatible with the purposes and principles of the Charter of the United Nations"?

**RUBRIC**

## Analyzing Bias in a First-hand Account

**Students will analyze the bias that exists in a first-hand account and how that bias shapes the opinions presented in the document. An exemplary analysis of bias in a document will meet the following criteria.**

- Identifies the main points presented in the first-hand account
- Offers an in-depth interpretation of the first-hand account
- Differentiates between facts and opinions
- Identifies and presents information about the writer
- Assesses the writer's reliability
- Determines the goals of the first-hand account
- Considers and assesses the writer's perspective
- Determines the writer's intended audience
- Describes the historical context for the time and place in which the account was created, and analyzes how this context might have shaped the opinions expressed in the document
- Infers what political or societal influences might have shaped the opinions presented in the document
- Determines whether the writer had first-hand knowledge on the topic or event, or whether he or she is reporting as a secondary source
- Determines the bias in the first-hand account
- Explores other sources related to the topic of the first-hand account to compare perspectives and facts

## Non-Self-Governing Territories (as of 2017)

The following territories are on the UN list of Non-Self-Governing Territories.

| Continent/ Geographical Region | Territory | Administering State | Legal Status |
|---|---|---|---|
| Africa | Western Sahara | Morocco<br>Spain<br>Sahrawi Arab Democratic Republic | Disputed |
| | St. Helena, Ascension and Tristan da Cunha | United Kingdom | Overseas Territory |
| Europe | Gibraltar | | |
| South America | Falkland Islands (Malvinas) | | |
| North America / Caribbean and Atlantic | Anguilla | | |
| | Bermuda | | |
| | British Virgin Islands | | |
| | Cayman Islands | | |
| | Montserrat | | |
| | Turks and Caicos Islands | | |
| Oceania / Pacific | Pitcairn Islands | | |
| | Tokelau | New Zealand | Territory |
| | French Polynesia | France | Overseas Collectivity |
| | New Caledonia | | Special Collectivity |
| | American Samoa | United States | Unincorporated Unorganized Territory |
| | Guam | | Unincorporated Organized Territory |
| North America / Caribbean | United States Virgin Islands | | |

declaration also says that "inadequacy of political, economic, social or educational preparedness should never serve as a pretext for delaying independence." This means that the administering nation should not try to keep control of the NSGT by using its poverty, for example, as an excuse.

### The Special Committee on Decolonization

The people who work the hardest at trying to help NSGTs become independent are those on the UN Special Committee on Decolonization. The United Nations created the Special

Committee to assist NSGTs in their quest for independence.

The Special Committee is sometimes called the Committee of 24 because it has 24 members. The job of the Special Committee is to study each NSGT and to write reports outlining the unique circumstances facing each territory. Then, the Special Committee makes specific recommendations about steps to be taken to move each territory closer to independence.

The Special Committee is also responsible for distributing information about decolonization, both to the people of administering nations and to those in NSGTs. The UN believes that when people in NSGTs learn about the United Nations, its Universal Declaration of Human Rights, and Resolution 1514, they are more likely to begin wanting self-government and work toward it themselves.

## Non-Self-Governing Territories Today

The United Nations keeps a list of all NSGTs. As of 2017, most of the 17 territories on the list are small islands in the Pacific Ocean or the Caribbean. The UN's goal is to have no territories on the list at all and have the current territories become self-governing.

Although dozens of NSGTs had gained independence with the help of the United Nations, by the 1980s, the process of decolonization had slowed down. The Special Committee on Decolonization decided it needed to rekindle interest in helping NSGTs achieve self-determination.

The Pitcairn Islands, one of the United Kingdom's overseas territories, is made up of four individual islands called Pitcairn, Henderson, Ducie, and Oeno.

**ACTIVITIES**

### First Hand

**Marking Fifty-Sixth Anniversary of Decolonization Declaration, Special Committee Calls on Member States to Help End Colonial Rule**

Examine the text of the official press release of the Special Committee.

1. How does this press release describe the work of the Special Committee? Why is the work of the committee described in these terms?
2. How would the addition of more member states representatives to the Special Committee help attain the goals of Resolution 1514? Propose some theories and discuss them.

### Where the Power Lies

Research why one of the NSGTs may want to become independent and compare it to the reasons why America wanted to gain its independence from Britain in the 1770s. Are there any differences? Are there any similarities? Create a table showing each.

RUBRIC

## Creating a Map

**Students will create a map of a relevant topic. An exemplary map will meet the following criteria.**

- Has a clearly distinguishable title (e.g., larger letters, underlines) that tells the purpose/content of the map
- Labels and locates all items correctly
- Includes a legend that is easy to find and contains a complete set of symbols, including a compass rose
- Scales all features correctly and clearly indicates the scale
- Uses correct spelling and capitalization
- Uses color appropriate for features (e.g., blue for water; black for labels)
- Includes properly documented sources

# Disputed Claims in Non-Self-Governing Territories Today

Of the 17 territories on the UN's list of Non-Self-Governing Territories, several are in dispute or have undergone recent change. Western Sahara, the Falkland Islands (Islas Malvinas), and Gibraltar have been the object of dispute concerning control by an administering state. French Polynesia has been added to the list of NSGTs as a result of disagreements between parties favoring and opposing increased self-governance.

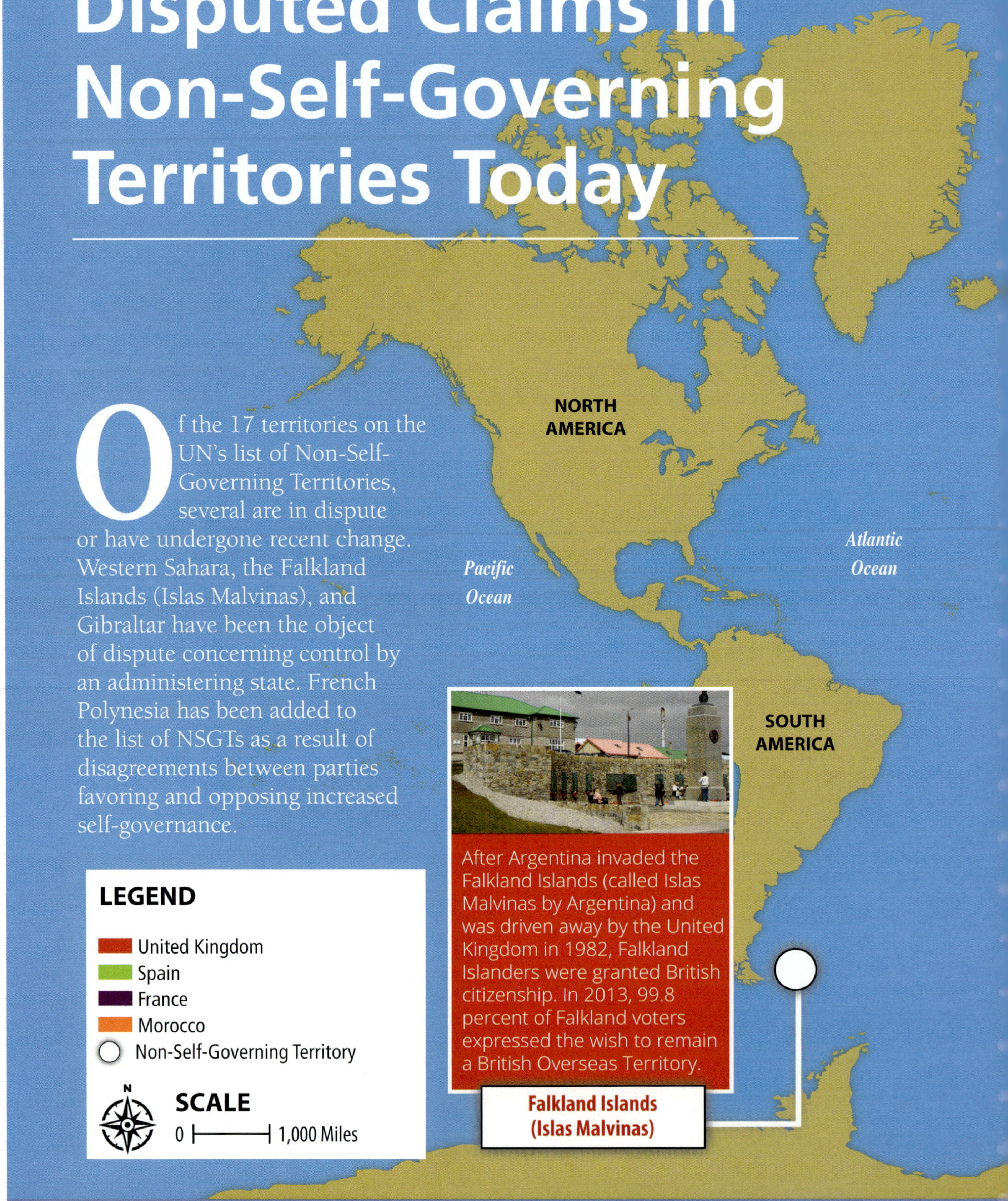

After Argentina invaded the Falkland Islands (called Islas Malvinas by Argentina) and was driven away by the United Kingdom in 1982, Falkland Islanders were granted British citizenship. In 2013, 99.8 percent of Falkland voters expressed the wish to remain a British Overseas Territory.

**Falkland Islands (Islas Malvinas)**

**LEGEND**

- United Kingdom
- Spain
- France
- Morocco
- Non-Self-Governing Territory

N

**SCALE**

0 — 1,000 Miles

## ACTIVITIES

### Google Maps

**Disputed Claims in Non-Self-Governing Territories Today.** Compare and contrast the situations of non-self-governing territories that are under dispute.

1. What do the disputes in these territories have in common? How do they differ? How could the UN intervene to solve these disputes?
2. In your opinion, other than to promote discussion of self-determination, why else might the UN have decided to reintroduce French Polynesia onto the list of non-self-governing territories in 2013?



**Gibraltar**

Gibraltar has long been under British rule. Over the years, several governments of Spain have challenged British claims to the territory. Following a war in the early 1700s, Spain gave up the territory. Since then, Spain has attempted to regain or influence control over Gibraltar.

**French Polynesia**

French Polynesia has been under French rule since the 1840s. In 2013, in order to promote discussion of self-determination, the UN added the region to its list of Non-Self-Governing Territories, making French Polynesia the most recent addition to the list.

**Western Sahara**

In 1975–1976, Spain gave up control of Western Sahara. Since then, Western Sahara has been the object of a dispute between Morocco and the Sahrawi Arab Democratic Republic, a government-in-exile. Each controls a portion of the territory.

# CHAPTER 4

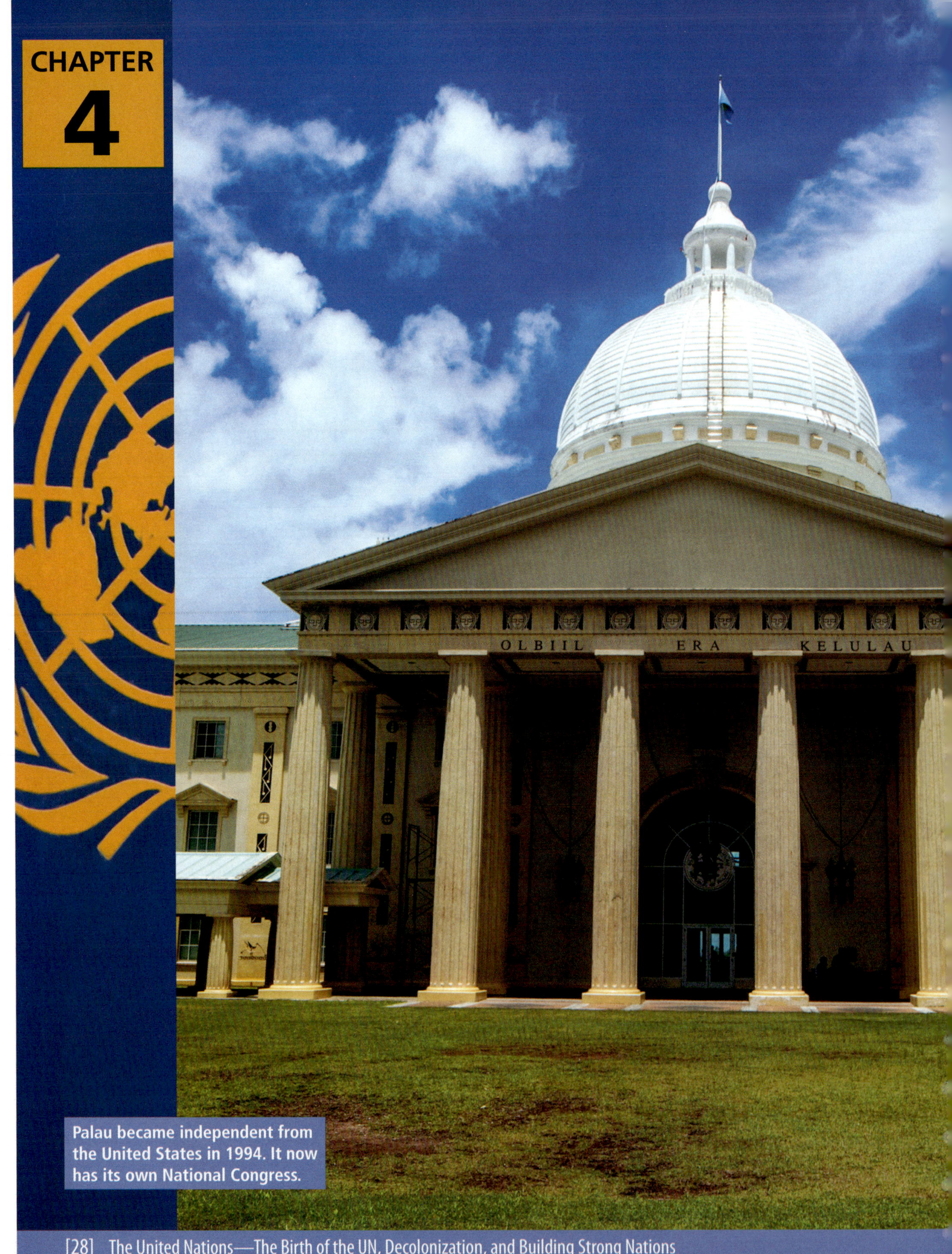


Palau became independent from the United States in 1994. It now has its own National Congress.

# The International Decades for the Eradication of Colonialism

In the late 1980s, the Special Committee on Decolonization decided something must be done to encourage the continuing process of helping Non-Self-Governing Territories become independent. Although many former colonies either had become independent nations—and members of the United Nations—or had freely chosen to associate themselves with other countries, the process had stalled. Progress toward self-determination in the remaining NSGTs had slowed dramatically, with little being done by the administering powers to help the territories work toward independence. The Special Committee suggested that a renewed emphasis on self-determination for all peoples would help reenergize the process.

**4**
The number of U.S.-administered territories that achieved self-governance during the International Decade for the Eradication of Colonialism, out of a total of 5 territories that became self-governing during the decade.

**1**
The number of territories that achieved self-governance during the Second International Decade for the Eradication of Colonialism (2001–2010).

**0**
The number of territories that have achieved self-governance during the Third International Decade for the Eradication of Colonialism (2011–2020).

**ACTIVITIES**

### Document

**Resolution adopted by the General Assembly on 10 December 2010**
Analyze the text of the resolution establishing the Third International Decade for the Eradication of Colonialism.

1. What is the purpose of the Third International Decade for the Eradication of Colonialism? Does it differ from the declared purpose of the first two decades? Why or why not?
2. Is the "Eradication of Colonialism" achievable by the end of 2020? Which measures can the UN take to ensure this goal is attained?

### Weblink

**Independence for Palau ends U.S. Sovereignty over Pacific Islands.**
Examine the context and events that led to Palau's independence from the United States.

1. In your opinion, why was the attainment of independence highlighted by a traditional ceremony?
2. Why would opponents challenge "the notion that Palau was gaining true independence"? Do you agree with their arguments? Why or why not?

## The International Decade for the Eradication of Colonialism

In 1988, the UN General Assembly proposed that the years between 1990 and 2000 be known as the International Decade for the **Eradication** of Colonialism. The goal of the decade would be "ushering in the twenty-first century, a world free from colonialism." Ideally, the United Nations wanted no territories remaining on the Non-Self-Governing Territories list by the end of the twentieth century.

To fulfill this goal, the United Nations, and especially the Special Committee, would have to work hard. Several things were needed to meet their objective. An essential part of ending colonialism was the cooperation of the administering powers. For territories to become self-governing, they needed the ongoing help and support of the countries governing them. Another important part of the process of self-determination was making sure the people of the territories had all the information they would need to make informed decisions. Since every

### Controversy in the Americas?

**Some people feel that the list of regions on the UN list of Non-Self-Governing Territories is debatable. It has been argued that some places on the list should be left off, and other places currently off the list should be included. Three of these places have ties to North America. Two not on the list—the Canadian province of Québec and the U.S. state of Hawai'i—have independence movements, and some believe they should be included on the list for this reason. Others think the United States Virgin Islands (designated an "unincorporated organized territory" of the United States) should not be included on the list, since the United States has tried to move the islands toward self-determination.**

**Québec**

**Hawai'i**

**United States Virgin Islands**

territory faced a different situation, studies also needed to be done on detailing specific actions that needed to be taken to move each territory closer to self-determination.

## Regional Seminars

One of the most obvious steps taken during the International Decade for the Eradication of Colonialism was the beginning of the regional seminars. Each year in May, seminars are held in either the Caribbean or the Pacific, alternating each year. Members of the Special Committee attend the seminars, as do delegates from the NSGTs and the administering countries. Representatives from other UN member countries and agencies often attend these seminars as well.

The regional seminars offer an opportunity for the NSGTs to each make presentations detailing the situations in their territories. Possible solutions and steps can be put forward and debated at the seminars. With the information gathered at these yearly meetings, policies and precise action plans can be created, giving steps to be taken in each territory to move it closer to self-determination.

**ACTIVITIES**

### More

**Controversies in the Americas?**
Analyze the situations of territories that should belong, or be removed, from the UN list of non-self-governing territories.

1. Do you think that territories seeking independence should have to belong to the UN list of non-self-governing territories? Defend your opinion.
2. What challenges are faced by newly independent countries?
3. Should territories that do not seek self-governing status remain on the UN's list? And would UN action to turn them into self-governing territories be a violation of their right of self-determination? Justify your answer.

The 2018 regional seminar was held in St. George's, Grenada, in the Caribbean.

## Results of the International Decade for the Eradication of Colonialism

As the 1990s drew to a close, it became clear the UN's goal of ending colonialism by the end of the millennium would not be achieved. Five territories had achieved self-determination, but this still left 17 on the Non-Self-Governing Territories list. The Special Committee felt they had made a great deal of progress in helping the territories and their administering nations take the necessary steps toward self-government, but obviously much more work still needed to be done.

One of the difficulties the Special Committee had encountered was getting the full cooperation of the administering nations. Some administering nations insisted that certain territories were happy remaining as colonies. This was true to some extent, since the tiny island territories appear to have greater economic advantages by

As a territory, Tokelau receives visits from New Zealand's government officials, such as the prime minister, so the administering power can have a better sense of what is happening in their territories.

staying as they are rather than choosing independence. As territories governed by wealthy administering nations, they have access to greater resources than they would if they were to try to survive on their own. This is especially true in the Caribbean, where all of the NSGTs are administered by either the United Kingdom or the United States. Many residents of these islands are comfortable with their lives and see no reason to change.

## Second and Third International Decades for the Eradication of Colonialism

In 1999, the UN General Assembly admitted they would not be able to eradicate colonialism by the twenty-first century as they had hoped. They proposed a Second International Decade for the Eradication of Colonialism, this one from 2001 to 2010, during which there was some success. In 2002, the Territory of East Timor, administered by Portugal, became independent as the country of Timor-Leste. This was a great victory for the United Nations, since many UN agencies worked together to bring about this independence.

In 2004, leaders of Tokelau, a Pacific territory administered by New Zealand, agreed to make Tokelau an associated state. This meant that Tokelau would become independent, and New Zealand would provide certain services to its former territory. In 2007, a majority of voters in Tokelau wanted their islands to become self-governing in free association with New Zealand. The vote fell short of the required two-thirds majority by 16 votes, however, and Tokelau remains a territory of New Zealand. If, and when, Tokelau comes off the NSGTs list, 16 territories will remain.

The Special Committee had been working hard to remove from the list as many of these territories as possible before the end of the Second International Decade for the Eradication of Colonialism in 2010. The circumstances facing each of these territories were unique and the challenges were great, which explains why independence for these territories has yet to come. However, the United Nations is not giving up and the Special Committee is still hard at work.

Hoping that more progress can be made, the United Nations has been holding regional seminars on the issue, and in 2011, set up the Third International Decade for the Eradication of Colonialism. The resolution was passed on December 10, 2010.

### Where the Power Lies

Imagine you are on the Special Committee for Decolonization. Choose a territory on the Non-Self-Governing Territories list. Research that territory and make a list of specific recommendations to help this territory become self-governing.

**ACTIVITIES**

**Weblink**

**Tokelau Government—Political System**

Analyze the political system adopted by the non-self-governing territory of Tokelau, and its interaction with New Zealand.

1. What elements of Tokelau's political system make it a non-self-governing territory? In which ways do these elements limit Tokelau's independence? Justify your answer.
2. How could the political system of Tokelau be reformed, should the territory receive full independence from New Zealand?

**RUBRIC**

## Analyzing a Current Events Video

**Students will watch and assess a video related to a current event, and write an analysis of the video. An exemplary video analysis will meet the following criteria.**

- Identifies the purpose of the video
- Identifies the intended audience of the video
- Identifies the video as a primary or secondary source
- Discusses the sociopolitical context of the video
- Describes how the content of the video is presented
- Summarizes the information and opinions presented in the video
- Analyzes the quality of the content presented in the video
- Assesses the effectiveness of the video
- Determines whether the images and graphics used in the video relate to the content
- Determines whether the video is easy to follow and understand
- Gives the analysis a clear and consistent purpose
- Organizes the analysis in a logical, effective manner
- Presents a strong, clear argument about the video
- Provides strong and accurate details to support the argument about the video
- Considers other perspectives on the purpose and effectiveness of the video
- Cites all sources used in the analysis

# CHAPTER 5

Puerto Ricans are divided on whether or not Puerto Rico should be independent. Those in favor of independence have protested in front of government buildings.

# Territories Helped by the Decolonization Process

Each territory that has achieved self-determination with the help of the United Nations has its own story. For some, a simple vote might have been all that was needed after the people of the territory received enough information to make an educated decision. Others faced war and years of hardships before they were ready to choose their own future.

## Namibia

Before it gained its independence in 1990, the country of Namibia was known as South West Africa. In the nineteenth century, South West Africa had been a German colony. Then, after World War I, the territory became a League

**1898**
The year that the United States acquired Puerto Rico and other lands from Spain. Today, Puerto Rico is a Commonwealth that belongs to the United States but is not a U.S. state.

**1960**
The year that 17 former African colonies, now independent nations, became members of the UN.

**2016**
The year that Morocco expelled more than 70 members of the UN peacekeeping operation in Western Sahara after the UN criticized Morocco's control over the territory.

**ACTIVITIES**

**Video**

**Puerto Rico's Protest Art Calls for the Island's Independence.**
Evaluate the means employed by some Puerto Ricans campaigning for independence.

1. Do you think the form of independence campaigning adopted by these activists is effective? Why or why not? In your opinion, why are paintings on public property sanctioned so severely? Is it related to the activists' work?
2. What are the arguments proposed to support Puerto Rican independence? Do you think these arguments are valid? Justify your answer.

**Weblink**

**Morocco Orders U.N. to Cut Staff in Disputed Western Sahara Territory**
Analyze the 2016 crisis in Western Sahara.

1. In your opinion, why did the Moroccan authorities take issue with the definition of Western Sahara as "an occupied region"?
2. What was the purpose of the Mission for the Referendum in Western Sahara, the members of which were expelled by the Moroccan government? Why were the members expelled? Is the reason suggested by the representative of the Polisario Front plausible? Why or why not?

Namibia's president named Saara Kuugongelwa-Amadhila the country's first female prime minister in 2015, 15 years after Namibia became independent.

of Nations Mandate administered by South Africa. With the end of World War II and the creation of the United Nations, most Mandates became Trust Territories under the Trusteeship System. South Africa, however, wanted to make South West Africa part of its own country instead of turning it over to the United Nations to become a Trust Territory. The United Nations refused, but South Africa began slowly strengthening its control in the territory. South West Africa became the longest-lasting League of Nations Mandate, since it did not go through the process of change other Mandates had after the creation of the United Nations. The regulations governing Mandates were much more relaxed than those governing Trust Territories or Non-Self-Governing Territories, and the emphasis on achieving self-determination was much less.

During the 1960s, a group called the South West African People's Organization (SWAPO) began carrying out **guerrilla**-style raids, fighting against South Africa for independence. The violence increased, and in 1966, the United Nations finally stepped in to manage the situation. The first step the United Nations took was to end the South African Mandate on South West Africa and to add the territory to the Non-Self-Governing Territories list. Then, a number of UN member countries—such as the United States, Britain, France, Canada, and West Germany—began pressuring South Africa to agree to help South West Africa take steps toward self-determination. South Africa agreed to accept SWAPO as the official representatives of South West Africa and to begin negotiations with them.

The next several decades were difficult in the territory. Angola, just to the north of South West Africa, gained independence from Portugal in 1975, but this move came in the middle of a civil war. The fighting in Angola spilled over into South West Africa, with SWAPO rebels hiding in Angola and South African troops invading to arrest them for terrorist actions. One faction of the Angolan war was supported by Cuban forces, while South Africa supported another, and a third was made up of internal Angolan forces.

By the late 1980s, both Cuba and South Africa had tired of the war in Angola. South West Africa could not develop into a functioning nation—or even a thriving territory of South Africa as that country had hoped—until the war ended. In 1988, Cuba and South Africa pulled their forces out of Angola. South Africa agreed to help South West Africa begin the process of independence.

In 1990, South West Africa created a **constitution**, held elections, and became the independent nation of Namibia. **Diplomatic** assistance by the United Nations was important in helping this change take place. If the United Nations had not decided to intervene in 1966, declaring South West Africa a Non-Self-Governing Territory rather than a Mandate of South Africa, the country of Namibia would probably not exist today. Although South Africa continued to try to take possession of South West Africa, it faced the opposition of both the United Nations and its powerful member nations and of SWAPO and the people of the future Namibia. Under these pressures, South Africa finally agreed to take the necessary steps toward Namibia becoming independent.

## Timor-Leste

In 2002, Timor-Leste moved from Non-Self-Governing Territory status to achieve self-government. Before its independence that year, the country of

**ACTIVITIES**

**Weblink**

**SWAPO Party—Historical Background**

Analyze the historical background that led to the formation of the SWAPO party in Namibia.

1. Do you agree with the statement, "the establishment of a political organization was the most appropriate and effective way of achieve genuine independence"? Why or why not?
2. What was the relationship of the SWAPO party with the United Nations? Why did SWAPO affirm that a vision of "the United Nations as some kind of savior" was illusory?
3. Why was a liberation through armed struggle considered the only alternative for the SWAPO party? What other means could SWAPO have used to fight for liberation?

Timor-Leste held an election in 2017. It was the first election since UN peacekeepers had left the country.

Timor-Leste was known as East Timor, part of a tiny island at the eastern tip of the Indonesian **archipelago**. East Timor had been a colony of Portugal since the sixteenth century, although its small size and considerable distance from Europe meant that Portugal did not pay much attention to it. In the mid-1970s, Portugal began preparing East Timor for independence, helping establish political parties and scheduling an election for 1976. As East Timor moved closer to independence, Indonesia and Australia became nervous. The most popular political party in East Timor was thought to be **Marxist**, and they worried a revolutionary Marxist government could destabilize the whole region. The United States, in the middle of the **Cold War** with communist nations, was also concerned.

In 1975, a small conflict broke out between the two major political parties in East Timor, with the losing side fleeing over the border into Indonesia, leaving the Marxist party, Fretilin, in control of the region. Several months later, East Timor declared itself independent, although this independence was not accepted by many countries, since it had simply been declared rather than established through the regular diplomatic process. Less than two weeks later, Indonesian forces invaded East Timor, with the private approval of governments such as the United States and Australia. During the invasion, tens of thousands of Timorese people were killed.

Indonesia's occupation of East Timor continued, with the United States and other countries contributing weapons, equipment, and training. Western nations, if they admitted their support, claimed they were trying to keep peace in East Timor, naming the 1975 conflict as evidence of civil war. The United Nations condemned the occupation, but was unable to take any action against it, since the United States, one of the permanent members of the Security Council, was able to **veto** any proposals.

Then, in 1991, two things happened that turned public opinion. Until this time, most people in the world did not think much about East Timor. In November, Indonesian forces opened fire in the capital of Dili on a crowd of Timorese who had gathered to mourn a murdered independence activist. Approximately 250 people were killed, and many more badly wounded. Many of the dead were children. As news of the massacre spread, people were horrified. The issue of East Timor was no longer hidden from the world.

The other event that took place in 1991 was the fall of the Soviet Union. With communism crumbling and the Cold War over, countries such as the United States could no longer claim to support Indonesia's actions out of fear of a communist uprising in an independent East Timor.

The international community began to put pressure on Indonesia to withdraw its forces from East Timor. Finally, in 1999, Indonesia agreed to hold a **referendum** in the territory, offering the Timorese a choice between independence and becoming a self-governing province of Indonesia. When the results of the referendum were in, 78.5 percent had voted for independence.

Indonesia struck back against East Timor's decision by raiding and attacking throughout the territory. After the United States threatened to take away its economic support of Indonesia, the country gave in at last. At the end of 1999, the United Nations took direct control of East Timor, preparing it for independence. The government was called the United Nations Transitional Administration for East Timor (UNTAET) and was led by Australia, with the help of several other UN member nations.

In 2002, East Timor drew up a constitution, held elections, and became officially independent as the nation of Timor-Leste on May 20. Four months later, the country became a member of the United Nations.

## Western Sahara

Western Sahara is the largest territory remaining on the Non-Self-Governing Territories list. Located in the harsh Sahara Desert in northwest Africa, the area is very sparsely populated. In 1963, the United Nations added the territory to the Non-Self-Governing Territories list. At that time, it was under Spanish control. In 1966, the United Nations made a resolution calling for a referendum to be held in Western Sahara to lead to self-determination.

**ACTIVITIES**

### Weblink

**The Power of the Vote: Timor-Leste's Election History**

Analyze the events related to the 1999 referendum in Timor-Leste.

1. Did the violence prior the 1999 referendum influence the vote results and voter turnout? Why or why not?
2. In your opinion, what is "the power of the vote"? Justify your answer and support it with examples.

Demonstrations supporting Western Sahara's independence have taken place in other countries, including Spain.

**RUBRIC**

## Analyzing a Conflict

**Students will research a conflict and analyze its causes from different social science perspectives. An exemplary analysis will meet the following criteria.**

- States a position on which factor played a primary role in causing a conflict and draws a conclusion about how studying this conflict helps us understand the causes of specific conflicts in the world today
- Provides reason(s) for the position supported by evidence
- Includes an evaluation of factors causing the conflict from three or more of the following social science perspectives:
    - Geographic
    - Political
    - Economic
    - Cultural
    - Sociological
    - Psychological
- Provides reason(s) for the evaluations supported by evidence
- Analyzes specific, relevant information from three or more primary sources
- Makes explicit references within the paper or presentation to four or more credible sources that provide relevant information
- Cites sources within the paper, presentation, or bibliography

Spain agreed to help prepare the region for self-government, but then, in 1975, signed an agreement with Morocco and Mauritania, both of which bordered on Western Sahara. The Madrid Agreement stated that Spain, Morocco, and Mauritania would jointly administer Western Sahara until its people chose to become self-governing. Although Spain soon left the area, Moroccan forces controlled the north part of the territory, and Mauritanian forces controlled the south. Many of the native people, known as Sahrawis, left the area during this time and fled to Algeria. In Algeria, the independence party, called the Polisario, set up a government-in-exile, the Sahrawi Arab Democratic Republic, claiming control over Western Sahara.

In 1979, Mauritania agreed to side with the Polisario and pull out of Western Sahara. In response, Morocco began building a fortified wall running diagonally through the territory. The Polisario now controls the smaller area south and east of the wall, and Morocco controls the rest. Throughout the 1980s, the Polisario fought a guerrilla war with Moroccan forces. Finally, in 1991, both sides agreed to accept a UN peace plan. The plan called for a cease-fire and a referendum. The referendum would offer the people of Western Sahara a choice between becoming an official province of Morocco and independence.

As of 2017, no referendum had taken place in Western Sahara. The difficulty has been in determining who is eligible to vote. After the ceasefire, Morocco began sending settlers into the territory. The question raised is whether these people should be allowed to vote on the future of a region they have lived in for only a short time. Morocco has also ignored the UN's requests for a referendum, since it claims such a vote would be unnecessary. The United Nations is still working hard to find an acceptable plan for the future of Western Sahara and a resolution to the conflicts between Morocco and the Polisario.

The UN Security Council has held many meetings regarding the status of Western Sahara.

In April 2014, the Security Council reaffirmed all its previous resolutions on Western Sahara and reiterated its call for all parties and neighboring states to find an acceptable solution to the decades-old problem.

## The Winding Path to Self-Determination

Clearly, the process of decolonization is not always simple. People and nations often have very different views as to the best future for a territory. These differences of opinion can lead to violence and also contribute to the unique situations facing each of the NSGTs on their way to self-determination.

### Where the Power Lies

Research and write about the typical life of a young person your age living today in Namibia, Timor-Leste, or Western Sahara.

**ACTIVITIES**

### Video

**Voices of Western Sahara**

Examine the situation of Western Sahara's population.

1. What are the main challenges faced by the Saharawi population? What has caused these challenges? How would ending the territorial dispute in Western Sahara help with these challenges?
2. Why does the speaker state that "education has been the drive to our peaceful resistance"? Do you agree with the importance of education in this specific context? Defend your opinion.

RUBRIC

## Creating a Timeline

**Students will explore a topic related to a historical event and create a timeline to present their research on historical events connected to this topic. An exemplary timeline will meet the following criteria.**

- Includes the most significant events pertaining to the topic to be compared and analyzed
- Includes interesting events
- Uses accurate information for all events, including date, location, and major details
- Orders the events in a chronological sequence
- Describes each event with accurate, vivid, and specific details
- Presents the topic from three or more perspectives
- Inspires the reader to ask thoughtful questions regarding the events and perspectives presented in the timeline
- Uses correct spelling, grammar, and punctuation
- Presents the timeline in a visually attractive and striking manner
- Presents the timeline in a neat, organized manner that is logical and easy to follow
- Uses creativity to present the timeline in an engaging manner
- Effectively communicates historical information relating to the topic
- Supports each event with reliable sources
- Includes a correctly formatted bibliography of all sources used to create the timeline

# Timeline

The United Nations has had much success in helping free territories from the control of colonial powers. Nonetheless, there is still work to be done to bring a small but important number of territories to the point where they can determine their own forms of government—and their futures.

**1960**

The United Nations issues two resolutions addressing the issues of granting self-determination and independence to colonial peoples and Non-Self-Governing Territories.

**1945**

The UN Charter is signed by 50 nations.

**1946**

One of the UN's principal bodies, the Trusteeship Council, is established to assure the administering of territories taken from defeated nations after World Wars I and II, as well as the safety of their inhabitants.

**1962**

The Special Committee on Decolonization is established.

The United Nations ends South Africa's Mandate over South West Africa, adding the territory to the Non-Self-Governing Territories list.

A renewed emphasis on decolonization is proposed, intending to bring about an end to colonialism by the end of the twentieth century.

With the last remaining UN Trustee Territory, the archipelago of Palau, becoming self-governing, the UN's Trusteeship Council holds its last meeting.

1963 | 1966 | 1988 | 1990 | 1994 | 2016

Western Sahara is added to the UN's Non-Self-Governing Territories list.

The International Decade for the Eradication of Colonialism begins.

UN Secretary General Ban Ki-Moon calls Morocco's control of territory in Western Sahara an "occupation."

## ACTIVITIES

### Transparency

**Timeline of the Birth of the UN, Decolonization, and Building Strong Nations**

Analyze important historic events relating to decolonization in different cultural, historical, and contemporary contexts.

1. Why might these events be featured in the timeline? What makes these events important?
2. How might people from different social or ideological groups have interpreted these events when they took place?
3. What effect did these events have on people from different social and political groups?
4. How might these events have shaped the world today? What sources can be used to illustrate these effects?
5. How might recent perspectives affect the way people interpret these events?

# Quiz

**1** **What were the League of Nations Mandates?**

**2** On what qualifications were the three different groupings of League of Nations Mandates based?

**3** **What was the purpose of the UN's Trusteeship Council?**

**4** **What countries make up the Trusteeship Council?**

**5** About how many people lived under colonial rule in Non-Self-Governing Territories in 1945, the year the UN was founded?

## 6

**True or false? One way a Non-Self-Governing Territory may achieve self-governance is to link itself with another independent country.**

## 7

What was Namibia known as before gaining its independence in 1990?

## 8

**What nation is in conflict with a government-in-exile over the administering and control of Western Sahara?**

## 9

Counting the disputed territory of Western Sahara, how many territories are on the current UN list of Non-Self-Governing Territories?

## 10

In what two parts of the world are most of the territories on the list of Non-Self-Governing Territories located?

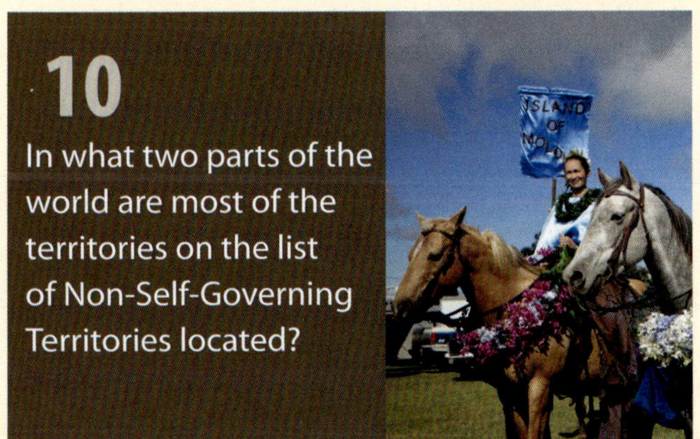

**ANSWERS**

**1** The colonies of defeated nations after World War I **2** How ready they were for self-governance **3** To look after the colonies of the defeated Axis powers after World War II, plus any remaining League of Nations Mandates **4** China, France, Russia, the United Kingdom, and the United States **5** 750 million **6** True **7** South West Africa **8** Morocco **9** 17 **10** The Caribbean and the Pacific

# Key Words

**Allied:** of or relating to the group of powers that fought against Germany in World War I or against the Axis powers in World War II

**archipelago:** a group or chain of islands

**Axis:** the military and political alliance of Germany, Italy, and Japan that fought the Allies in World War II

**Cold War:** a largely nonviolent conflict between capitalist and communist countries following World War II

**commonwealth:** a political unit having local autonomy but voluntarily united with the United States

**constitution:** an official document outlining the rules of a system or government

**decolonization:** the act of granting a colony its independence

**delegates:** individuals chosen to represent or act on behalf of an organization or government

**diplomatic:** having to do with international negotiations without resorting to violence

**economic sanctions:** coercive measures—such as refusing to import a nation's products—adopted to force a nation violating international law to stop its actions

**epidemics:** widespread occurrences of infectious disease within a community at a particular time

**eradication:** the complete elimination of something so that it cannot recur or return

**factions:** smaller groups within larger groups that have opposing ideas

**free association:** a relationship between two independent nations or states in which the larger state may provide certain services or protections to the smaller one

**guerrilla:** describing a type of warfare conducted by independent units using surprise and sabotage

**human rights:** rights that everyone has, regardless of birthplace or citizenship

**Mandates:** in this context, territories for which the League of Nations members were given administrative powers

**Marxist:** someone who follows the political and economic theory of Karl Marx, who saw class struggle as the force behind change in Western society

**ratified:** formally approved something

**referendum:** a vote of the entire electorate on a question or questions put before it by the government or similar body

**refugees:** people who have been forced to leave their country in order to escape war, persecution, or natural disaster

**self-determination:** the power of a people or territory to establish its own form of government

**self-government:** the governing, or administering, of a country, state, or territory by its own people, especially after having been a colony

**trusteeship:** the authority of a country or other governmental entity to administer a territory, region, or country

**Trust Territories:** territories under the trusteeship or authority of the United Nations or of a country designated by the UN

**unanimous:** relating to a situation in which all members agree

**veto:** to exercise the power of a person, country, or branch of government to reject the legislation of another

# Index

# LIGHTBOX

## SUPPLEMENTARY RESOURCES

Click on the plus icon ⊕ found in the bottom left corner of each spread to open additional teacher resources.

- Download and print the book's quizzes and activities
- Access curriculum correlations
- Explore additional web applications that enhance the Lightbox experience

## LIGHTBOX DIGITAL TITLES
### Packed full of integrated media

**VIDEOS**

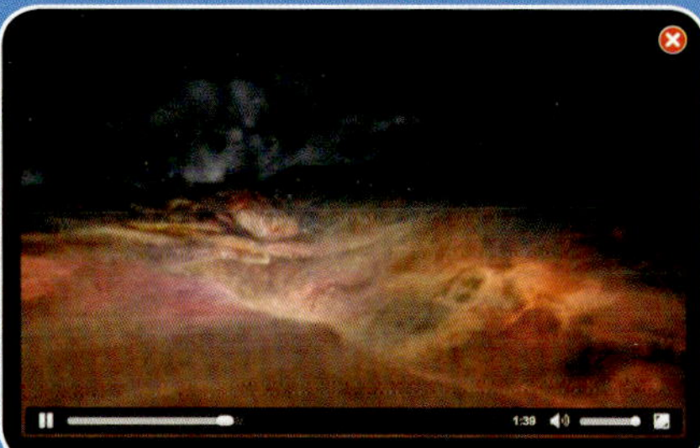

**INTERACTIVE MAPS**

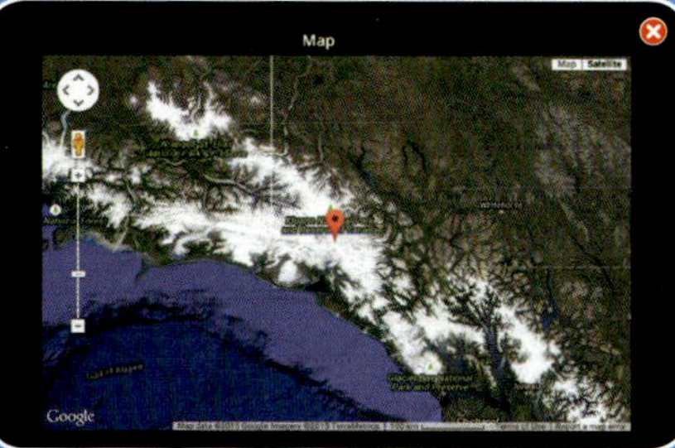


**WEBLINKS**

**SLIDESHOWS**

**QUIZZES**

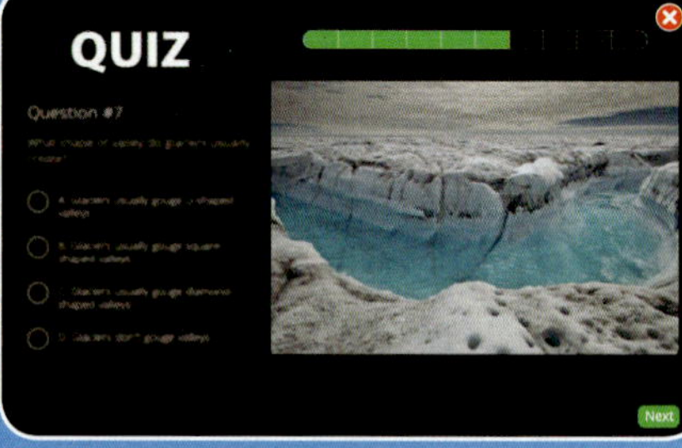


## OPTIMIZED FOR

- ✓ TABLETS
- ✓ WHITEBOARDS
- ✓ COMPUTERS
- ✓ AND MUCH MORE!

Published by Smartbook Media Inc.
350 5th Avenue, 59th Floor New York, NY 10118
Website: www.openlightbox.com



First published by Mason Crest in 2016

Library of Congress Control Number: 2018941522

ISBN 978-1-5105-3967-9 (hardcover)
ISBN 978-1-5105-3968-6 (multi-user eBook)

Printed in Brainerd, Minnesota, United States
1 2 3 4 5 6 7 8 9 0 22 21 20 19 18

072018
121217

**Project Coordinator:** Heather Kissock
**Designer:** Nick Newton

Every reasonable effort has been made to trace ownership and to obtain permission to reprint copyright material. The publisher would be pleased to have any errors or omissions brought to its attention so that they may be corrected in subsequent printings.

The publisher acknowledges Getty Images, Alamy, and iStock as its primary image suppliers for this title.